Job Interview Questions & Answers

Your Guide to Winning in Job Interviews

Liz Cassidy

Liz Cassidy
Third Sigma International
Level 7, 320 Adelaide St
Brisbane
QLD 4000
Australia.
www.lizcassidy.com

This publication is designed to provide general accurate and authoritative information in regard to the subject matter covered. It is sold the understanding that the publisher is not engaged in rendering legal, accounting, or other specific professional services. If legal advice or other expert assistance is required, the services of a competent professional person should be sought.

Go to page 97 to get Liz Cassidy's personal help with your career

Contents

Go to page 97 to get Liz Cassidy's personal help with your career

Dedication

I dedicate this book to my inspirational husband,
Richard.

Thanks Honey.

Go to page 97 to get Liz Cassidy's personal help with your career

About the Author

Liz Cassidy, #1 Amazon Best Selling Author & founder of the Leadership Mastery Institute and Third Sigma International, is a Leadership Coach and Speaker.

With 27 years industry and business experience in multinational, nationals and small business, in the UK and Australia within Production, Operations, Distribution Management, Sales and Professional Services in traditional and online businesses, there are not many aspects of Building, Leading and Managing a Business that Liz has not experienced.

Now Brisbane based she travels to the USA extensively with her business and is recognized and acknowledged for her skill and ability in assisting her Executive Coaching clients to overcome business and leadership blocks.

Liz has been a guest on local and national radio and has been featured in a number of business magazines. she has a Bachelor of Science - Chemical Engineering.

Go to page 97 to get Liz Cassidy's personal help with your career

Go to page 97 to get Liz Cassidy's personal help with your career

Chapter 1

Congratulations

You have just bought the book which will put you in prime position to win in your job interview.

Being prepared for a job interview is essential when you want to get the right role for you.

Getting prepared for the interview is a project which needs some planning and investment of your time and your patience.

Reading and using this book is your first step to being totally prepared for your new career.

I am constantly amazed at how sloppy, under-prepared and naive some people are when it comes to job interviews. This is a critical step in changing or progressing in your career – please don't leave it to chance.

I have written this book for you as a direct result of my work in career transition coaching, and in assisting my leadership clients to prepare for interviews - both internal and external. I love seeing my clients go from stress and disappointment to getting what they

Go to page 97 to get Liz Cassidy's personal help with your career

specifically wish for and deserve in their careers. And with a little thought and preparation you can have exactly that too.

When you do your advance research and you are fully prepared for your interview you can be more relaxed during the meeting itself. You will be more natural; less stressed and you can allow your innate personality to shine.

When you are prepared for your interview - it shows.

The interviewer can also relax more. So your interview will progress as a normal business meeting and will be less effort for all concerned.

When you read through the following pages I urge you to make notes on how you want to adapt the answers to the questions so that your own strengths shine through. Then, practice your answers out loud a few times, so that on the day you won't have to hunt for answers. They will come naturally - but not as if you have rehearsed them.

Then, you can meet your new employer as his absolute best candidate and as the solution to his problems.

Good luck.

Go to page 97 to get Liz Cassidy's personal help with your career

Chapter 2

Know Your Interviewer

Before we get into the detail of preparing you for your interview, put yourself into the shoes of the person who will be conducting your interview.

Aside from professional recruiters, the majority of business owners and managers have NEVER had any interview skills training.

Managers and Business Owners

Your role is to make his job easier. By that I mean - make it easy for him to choose you. The more prepared you are, the less stress you will be putting on him.

Make it a relief to have you sitting in front of him.

He is doing the best he can with very little training or preparation.

Imagine if you will what the life of your interviewer is like.

He is understaffed, (after all he is recruiting for this role), he is probably putting in too many hours at

Go to page 97 to get Liz Cassidy's personal help with your career

work already, and now he has to take time out of his already overloaded life to interview when he just wants to be back at his desk fighting the fires he knows are smouldering in his absence.

It's not a pretty thought is it?

Then you turn up to your interview with your research done, answers prepared and show that you are just the right person to make his life easier. He will compare you to someone else who may not have well thought out answers or questions; who may bumble and stumble their way through the interview process making it agony for all concerned. At worst he will be grateful to you; at best....he may just offer you the job.

The Owner or Manager will likely be strong technically and will want to talk shop about his problems and potential solutions. He will want to know if you are competent and professional, and if you fit in. (i.e. Does he like you?) He may have prepared some standard questions and will work mainly from résumé. Thus the questions you are asked may not be the same questions other candidates are asked. He may be comparing apples and pears.

He may want to tell you how he built the business and will give you some history. He may want you to be a change agent, replacing the old ways to lift his

Go to page 97 to get Liz Cassidy's personal help with your career

business unit to "the next level". He may also want you to meet his senior team to get their support.

The person interviewing you has problems. Treat this as an opportunity to assist and be of service. Also treat this as an opportunity to learn more about this person who may well be your future boss and about how he handles stress.

Professional Recruiters

Many, but not all, professional recruiters are formally trained in behavioural interview skills. Don't make assumptions about the quality of the interview you are about to have - be prepared for a great interviewer, just as you are prepared for an inexperienced interviewer.

Professional Recruitment firms are usually paid on commission. They also guarantee the performance of whoever they place into the position. If they have to make a replacement, then they lose time and money. They want to make sure they have the best person available in a limited time to make a short-list of interviewees for their client. No short-list - no placement - no commission. They won't have much time to spend with you in your interview so they will be searching for evidence that you could make their short-list. Most professional recruiters will make this task easy for you.

Go to page 97 to get Liz Cassidy's personal help with your career

Professional recruiters put their client's top candidate requirements into their job advert. Recruiters are quite ruthless in sorting applications and resumes into their 'Yes' and 'No' piles. If your application does not meet their specific criteria then you will go into the 'No' pile. When you get into the 'Yes' pile then you are likely to get a first interview. In this screening interview they will want to verify that they have made the right choice in investing time meeting you. They will also be looking for a good cultural fit with their client. Again they will be ruthless in sorting Yes and No candidates.

You will make the recruiter's life easier if you have researched the client (if possible) and show that you are flexible, skilled and able to impress within a few minutes of meeting.

Internal Recruiters

Internal recruiters generally work for large organizations, and their role is to recruit just for that organization. They are usually on salary and the pressures of their role are different from the professional external recruiter or the manager who is short staffed. The internal recruiter is satisfying the needs of an internal stakeholder, and may well be looking for career progression as a result of performance in their role.

Go to page 97 to get Liz Cassidy's personal help with your career

Many internal recruiters, but not all, are recent Human Resources graduates. This may well be their first experience of working for a large organization.

Go to page 97 to get Liz Cassidy's personal help with your career

Go to page 97 to get Liz Cassidy's personal help with your career

Chapter 3

Types of Interviews

Although most of your interviews will be one-on-one, there may be some group interviews. Managers pressed for time can find group interviews efficient.

Some organizations can require a presentation in front of a group of future colleagues as part of the interview process. It allows the interview team to evaluate candidates' communication ability, influencing skills and ability to think on their feet.

There are two basic types of interviews - informational interviews and selection interviews.

The informational interview can be a formal or informal conversation for the purpose of obtaining information to determine further courses of action.

The selection interview is a planned, formal, more focused conversation that provides the interviewer with the information to evaluate whether or not a candidate has the ability and motivation to perform successfully and fit into the organization.

Go to page 97 to get Liz Cassidy's personal help with your career

Selection interviews may be screening interviews by search company professionals, internal Human Resources professionals, or the ultimate hiring manager. The purpose of these interviews is to screen you in or out, based on predetermined qualification criteria.

A selection interview can be either structured or unstructured.

The questions asked at your interview will tell you the sub-plot of the current organization, its culture and the challenges you will be facing.

Structured Interviews

The structured interview is exactly what it sounds like - an interview that is conducted according to a predetermined order. It is (usually) carefully designed to elicit maximum data from the candidate with a minimum number of interviewer questions. The structure will usually follow the outline below:

- Greetings / small talk
- Your work experience
- Your education
- Activities and interests
- Summary of strengths and weaknesses

Go to page 97 to get Liz Cassidy's personal help with your career

- Role specific stretch and discovery questions
- Description of position, candidate questions
- Close.

The trained interviewer conducting a structured interview will be likely to do the following:

Ask open ended questions and focus on your past performance.

Encourage you to talk 70-80 per cent of the time.

Give you limited specific information about the job until your qualifications have been confirmed.

Maintain eye contact.

Be comfortable with silences and wait for you to speak.

Not ask personal or inappropriate questions.

Unstructured Interviews

Unstructured interviews are non-directed and are geared to be more casual and open. Often the

Go to page 97 to get Liz Cassidy's personal help with your career

interviewers have had little or no training or coaching about the process, and have done little to prepare.

These can be difficult situations, particularly when the interviewer does not know what to look for or how to direct the interview. It is important for you to take the initiative and lead without appearing to dominate – the person asking the questions usually controls the conversation.

Screening Interviews

Screeners may be outside parties such as recruitment consultants, employment agency representatives, or even an independent psychologist. Often these interviewers are more expert in extracting information and evaluating people than the company interviewer who will eventually make a decision about you.

Larger companies have internal screening interviewers who sort out applicants and candidates, deciding whether to pass them along to the decision makers. These screeners are usually from the Human Resources unit. Keep in mind that although they cannot hire you, they can eliminate you from consideration.

Go to page 97 to get Liz Cassidy's personal help with your career

Sequential Interviews

These are a series of interviews scheduled one after another at specific intervals over a period of time (one day or a half day). Sequential interviews can be conducted with a reporting chain of supervisors, peers or team members.

It is important to consider each new interviewer as the most important person you are meeting. Adapt your style to suit each new interviewer, listen actively and give considered responses. You may find that there is little coordination among the interviewers and they will ask you the same questions over and over again. Sometimes this is done deliberately, to check the consistency of your answers.

Panel Interviews

These are interviews conducted by a number of interviewers (usually three to five) in the same room at the same time. In addition to saving time, consensus can be developed by simultaneously obtaining a number of interviewer reactions.

Here you will need to make each individual feel that you are paying particular attention to him. Be sure to maintain eye contact as you address each one, and try

Go to page 97 to get Liz Cassidy's personal help with your career

to match the personality style of each to communicate with each in a way that he is likely to respond to.

Interviews with Decision Makers

These interviews are with your future manager. If you have done well with the screeners and other interviewers, you will have some positive momentum when you meet the decision maker, as a favourable evaluation will precede you.

Stamp of Approval Interviews

These are final interviews with company directors and other senior executives usually for more senior or critical roles. While the hiring decision may already have been made, this is an opportunity for senior executives to meet potential new members of staff.

Stress Interview

In this situation, the interviewer deliberately creates a charged atmosphere. He may contradict or argue with you, change conversational course without warning; and use other techniques to create tension. These interviews are rare, thankfully.

Go to page 97 to get Liz Cassidy's personal help with your career

The interviewer who chooses to conduct a stress interview is rarely a trained interviewer. However, he is likely to be the decision maker who wants to ascertain how you will handle stress. (Consider the possibility that a "stress interviewer" may also be a "stress creator").

Presentation Interview

Some organizations will ask you to make a formal presentation on a selected topic as part of your interview process.

This is also rare, but in the event that it does happen, remember to minimize the use of PowerPoint slides and to practice your presentation in advance with an honest reviewer.

Go to page 97 to get Liz Cassidy's personal help with your career

Go to page 97 to get Liz Cassidy's personal help with your career

Chapter 4

Developing Your Interview Skills

Studying and learning about the interview process, combined with practice, will help you to handle interviews well.

Rehearsing by yourself and practising with others will help you to plan for and simulate the actual encounters. Although you may feel a little awkward practising this way initially, you will notice a substantial improvement in a short time.

If possible, video or record yourself in a practice interview.

Work with someone you feel comfortable with and have him or her ask you questions as if in an interview. You can obtain valuable feedback and will be able to make improvements once you see yourself on video. You may be put off by the initial impact of seeing yourself on screen, and the sooner you get over this awkwardness the faster you can develop your skill. Most people, even TV performers, hate to see themselves on screen.

Go to page 97 to get Liz Cassidy's personal help with your career

It has been my experience that this type of practice will help you to build on your strengths and highlight areas for improvement, so that you will be prepared for actual interview situations.

Preparing and Practicing

To sharpen your interview interaction skills:

> Review any previous assessment results, accomplishments, skills, profiles and your résumé.

> Study the interview questions that follow later in this book and plan how you would respond to each. Take notes so that your preparation can be finessed.

> Practise by yourself and with a partner and with audio or video recording.

> Research the company, functional area, department, or interviewer(s) prior to the interview. There is more information available online than you could imagine. Use it.

Go to page 97 to get Liz Cassidy's personal help with your career

Your 2 Minute Introduction

Your 2 Minute Introduction is the first step in interview preparation. During an interview, you will probably be responding to the question "Tell me about yourself".

The best response to that question is with one of your own: "Where would you like me to begin?" The listener might want you to start at one of the following places:

Where you were born and raised.

Where you received your education.

After school / university.

When you accepted your first position - or

They will ask you to decide.

When dealing with the first three items above, plan to spend about 30 seconds. When you begin discussing your career history, give a more detailed, chronological description, beginning with your early highlights and working up to the present day. Minimize the details of your earlier work and be more expansive about your last positions, the ones in which you were likely to have made the most significant contributions. (This will hold true unless you are

Go to page 97 to get Liz Cassidy's personal help with your career

changing careers, and wish to refer back to an earlier, more appropriate position.) This should take about one to one and a half minutes.

Be succinct and practice this with a stop watch.

The tell me about yourself question is your opportunity to impress and engage early.

Next comes your question:

"Does that answer your question?", or

"Is there anything else?", or

"Would you like me to elaborate on any points?"

Moving on ...

In the event that you don't currently have a job and in response to the possible question, "Why did you leave your last company?" you can reply, "As you probably know, the company…"

Decided to relocate, and I chose not to move with them.

Has been reorganising for the past several months, and I have decided to explore other opportunities.

Go to page 97 to get Liz Cassidy's personal help with your career

Or, you can state whatever is appropriate in your case. Do not dwell on your response or provide a lot of detail, and remember to maintain eye contact with the interviewer.

Go to page 97 to get Liz Cassidy's personal help with your career

Go to page 97 to get Liz Cassidy's personal help with your career

Chapter 5

Marketing "You!"

During the interview process, you will be marketing your unique self as if you are a product or business.

However, you will be examining the company / interviewer as a potential customer.

In this context, keep in mind that the following Sales 101 points will help to increase your success as a candidate:

> Understand your customer's needs and expectations.
>
> Know your product and the benefits it will provide.
>
> Solve the customer's problems.
>
> Provide added value and become a resource.

Go to page 97 to get Liz Cassidy's personal help with your career

Managing Your Image

Since you will have only one opportunity to make that all-important first impression, keep the following in mind.

Physical presence. Dress appropriately for the culture where you are being interviewed, and, when in doubt, dress on the conservative side. Be sure your grooming and hygiene are immaculate.

Assume a posture that is neither too relaxed nor sloppy, nor too tense and forward. Leave any overcoats umbrellas etc. or large bags/ luggage outside the interview room. Take a notebook with your prepared questions and a pen (which works) into the room with you.

Movements and mannerisms. Use natural gestures. No matter how nervous you are do not clench your fists. Avoid fidgeting, scratching or fussing with objects such as pen, glasses, or change in your pocket. Move naturally – avoid looking stiff and awkward or slouching.

Go to page 97 to get Liz Cassidy's personal help with your career

Manner of speaking. Make sure you can be heard – be aware of the interviewer's reaction to your voice. Do not mumble or drop your voice to a whisper towards the end of your sentences. Avoid sing song or monotonous recitations, which will give the impression that you are over rehearsed.

Also, avoid slang and colloquialisms like "You know", as well as grunts, "like", "er", "um", "mate" etc.

Demeanour. Be enthusiastic, warm, and sincere to suit the dynamic of your interviewer. Be positive in your language, avoid negative topics and don't vent hostility. Smile!

Listening skills. Listen with full concentration and maintain eye contact 90 per cent of the time (without staring). Indicate attention and acceptance with nods and smiles, avoid interrupting. Be comfortable with silence when you need to think.

Communication skills. Mirror the style and pace of your interviewer. Answer forthrightly and credibly, and stop when you have answered the question. Don't

Go to page 97 to get Liz Cassidy's personal help with your career

over-elaborate with details or anecdotes, don't ramble or interrupt. If you don't know something, say so.

Clarify a question if you don't understand it. If you truly didn't understand the question, ask "Could you ask that question again, please, perhaps a different way"?

Listen before you talk and think before you speak.

Names. Get names and exact titles of your interviewers. Ask for company or departmental needs early in the interview using open-ended questions. Weave in your strengths and accomplishments in response to those needs. Respond to doubts or objections positively without being defensive.

Go to page 97 to get Liz Cassidy's personal help with your career

The Basics

Some basic interviewing principles to keep in mind.

Explore their needs. Remember that all successful selling starts with identifying the needs of the buyer, whether a company or a manager. Therefore, before you launch into your "carefully prepared story", try to get your interviewer talking about the position and the problems facing his or her company or department.

Listen actively! Feel free to take notes. This will give you something to relate to.

Show that you are a team player. Remember that your interviewer needs to be convinced that you will be liked and respected by all members of the team. A future manager will be considering what it would be like to have you around for a few years.

Be inquisitive. You are not only to answer, but to ask questions. You need to find out enough about the work, company, manager, and environment to convincingly demonstrate why you would be a valuable asset.

Go to page 97 to get Liz Cassidy's personal help with your career

An employment decision is a mutual commitment, so you owe it to yourself and your potential employer to explore how the organization and the position meet both of your needs.

Use silence to your advantage. Some interviewers are trained to create silent moments to get you to talk. Silences of ten seconds can seem like an eternity. Be aware of contrived silences and don't feel pressured to fill the gaps - simply stop and let them ask you more questions.

Wrap things up. When you sense your time is running short, try to get closure and ask what should happen next in the recruitment process. Try to establish a reason for further contact.

Chemistry

Chemistry in this context means how people interact and affect each other as they talk, exchange thoughts and feelings, and build a relationship. Chemistry is partly a function of personality, style, agendas and needs of both you and the interviewer. Be prepared for a wide variety of interviewer styles and agendas.

Go to page 97 to get Liz Cassidy's personal help with your career

When you can identify the interviewer's communication style, you can tailor your responses to meet their needs and expectations.

However, it is also important to listen to what is being said and to present YOU at your best.

Go to page 97 to get Liz Cassidy's personal help with your career

Go to page 97 to get Liz Cassidy's personal help with your career

Chapter 6

Your Ideal Job

During the interview process, you have the opportunity to match what the company has to offer with what you feel Your Ideal Job requirements are and whether or not these basic tangible and intangible criteria can be met by the position specifications and the company culture on offer.   The more time you spend in advance thinking about what your ideal job may be, the better you will be able to assess you best fit for this role, and the organization's best fit for your needs.

Pay particular attention to your responses to interview questions when evaluating the match.

One area which many candidates miss when researching a company and a role is the company culture and values set.

When you know your own values intimately then you will know whether a company will suit you and whether it will be a good fit. If their values are significantly different from yours; you will not enjoy the role and may suffer stress.

Go to page 97 to get Liz Cassidy's personal help with your career

The roles of values in creating a happy work environment cannot be overstated. Make sure you are very clear on what your work values are before you go for an interview. If you are unclear of your values you can use the resource on Page 97 to get more clarity.

Interview Tips

Try to recognize the type of interview quickly and respond accordingly.

Listen carefully to every question and be sure you understand it before answering. If necessary, rephrase and request clarification.

If there is an opportunity to take control of the interview by getting the interviewer to talk, do so - it gives the impression that you are a good listener, and you can learn a great deal about the interviewer and the company. However make sure that you don't dominate the interview.

Try to elicit specific job criteria from the interviewer early on, then you can gear your responses to meet those criteria.

Maintain external calm in a stress interview or when you are asked questions that you consider to be inappropriate.

Go to page 97 to get Liz Cassidy's personal help with your career

The more embarrassing or sensitive a question is, the shorter your answer should be. For example, if an interviewer asks why you were let go/retrenched, it is better to deal with this question briefly and respond with: "Our industry had been experiencing tough economic times, and my company had to eliminate many positions - including mine", then stop.

After you answer any question, stop.

Do not embellish, elaborate or ramble. If you don't know the answer, be honest and say so. Use silence to your advantage.

If asked behavioural, "what did you do?" questions, take time to think about the situation before answering. This gives you time to seriously consider the question, and also allows you a few moments to reduce your stress level.

Behavioral Interviews

Behavioural interviews are designed on the basis of "the best indicator of future performance is past behaviour"

The majority of professional recruiters will use Behavioural Interview techniques.

Go to page 97 to get Liz Cassidy's personal help with your career

A trained behavioural interviewer will ask you questions about how you behaved in certain circumstances, and will then analyse your answers on the basis of how he thinks you will behave in this role.

The questions asked in a behavioural interview are a very strong indicator of the skills and attributes needed for the role.

For example, I once asked a potential construction manager what his experience was in dealing with a difficult boss. After chuckling at the question, he responded with …"Just how difficult are we talking about?" He got the hint, and the job.

Go to page 97 to get Liz Cassidy's personal help with your career

Hypothetical Interviews

Generally, untrained or inexperienced interviewers will ask questions about "How would you approach … (a situation)?"

This hypothetical style of question only tests your possible imagination, not your past performance or potential future success.

If you are asked a hypothetical question, acknowledge it politely then answer with…"What I did when I had that situation in the past was….. … So that is what I would do if faced with the same situation again."

The more specific you can be in your answer the more believable you are as a candidate.

In this way you are giving them evidence that you are experienced and that you can handle the role easily.

Go to page 97 to get Liz Cassidy's personal help with your career

Difficult Questions

Even if the intent is not to provoke stress, you will probably encounter some challenging questions.

Today there is a trend among interviewers to ask behavioural questions about how you handled certain work situations in the past. You might also be asked what you would do in a hypothetical work situation. While you cannot prepare specific answers to every behavioural or hypothetical question, review your accomplishments so that you can demonstrate that you possess the skills in question.

You might encounter any combination of the interview questions on the following pages, some of which may seem inappropriate. Try not to take any of these inappropriate questions personally or be offended. Responding with grace or with a question expressed pleasantly and without belligerence can prevent an awkward deadlock.

If you conscientiously practise answering the following questions, you will be prepared for most interviews. Practice with an audio recorder, and video a practise interview. We have suggested ways to respond to each question. However, there is no substitute for your own good judgement in determining how best to respond in an actual interview.

Go to page 97 to get Liz Cassidy's personal help with your career

Chapter 7

Social Media and Job Interviews

No matter what you think, your life is no longer private if you have a social media presence.

A well prepared interviewer will search for you online to find out more about you and to assess the truth and veracity of your resumé, and your fit for his business.

Assume that your interviewer has done this and be prepared for questions about any gaps or non-alignment between your online "self" and your resume.

Does your online brand present you as a serious candidate for this role, or does it sabotage your career chances? While you may enjoy a full and varied social life does your online brand present an extreme form or only one part of that life? If so, your interviewer may reach a conclusion about you *based on how you present yourself online.*

If you are serious about your career, clean up your online brand and ensure that your online and personal brand are aligned. Present yourself online and offline as someone this organization would be proud to have

Go to page 97 to get Liz Cassidy's personal help with your career

as a staff member. It is not just celebrities who have their careers derailed by a photograph of an ill-thought act posted online.

Some organizations have asked for passwords to cross-check the contents of an online profile with strong privacy settings. Without getting into the (il)legalities of this request; consider if this is the kind of organization you would want to work for.

Better still, if your profile and total web history is congruent with how you want to present yourself then you can invite your interviewer to connect online on a professional social website such as LinkedIn.

Go to page 97 to get Liz Cassidy's personal help with your career

Chapter 8

Types of Questions

Question can be split into types.

"Can Do" questions test if you can do the role.

"Will Do" questions test your attitude and willingness to get on with the role

"Best Fit" questions test whether you are the type of person who will fit into the team and organization.

"Stress" questions test how you will behave under stress. They are thankfully rare.

"Curve ball" questions are just that. All they provide is insight into your ability to handle awkward moments politely and your ability to think on your feet.

"Inappropriate" questions are those which have no place in an interview. However they do get asked. So being ready for them will help you get through an awkward moment with tact and diplomacy.

Go to page 97 to get Liz Cassidy's personal help with your career

Responses to Interview Questions

"Can Do" Questions

What can you offer us (that other candidates cannot)?

> Respond by emphasising your unique qualities and capabilities. Relate them to the position at hand whenever possible.

What are your strengths?

> You should be able to enumerate three or four of your key strengths (with examples) that are relevant to their needs, based on your research and other data you have gathered about the company.

How successful have you been so far?

> Be prepared to define success for yourself and then respond. Try to choose accomplishments that relate to the organization's needs and values if you have been able to determine that from your research.

> **What are your limitations?** Or Tell me about a time your work was critical. What was your biggest mistake?

Go to page 97 to get Liz Cassidy's personal help with your career

A response about a strength, which, if overdone, could be considered a weakness, can cause a problem. Professionals in most organizations are familiar with this technique and may consider it to be evasive. When discussing mistakes and criticism, emphasize what you learned and how your behaviour is different as a result of the experience.

Do not claim to be faultless.

What qualifications do you have that you feel would make you successful here?

If this question is asked after you have sufficient information about the position, talk about two or three of your major skills (supported by accomplishments), which you believe will be useful in the position. If the question is asked early on, talk about two or three of your major skills and, to the extent you can, relate them to the company.

How long would it take you to make a meaningful contribution to our firm?

More and more companies are looking for people who can "hit the ground running". They don't have time to bring people "up to speed" with on the job training. Again, the timing of

Go to page 97 to get Liz Cassidy's personal help with your career

the question is important. Do you know enough about the specific position to give a sensible response? If so, think about your accomplishments and select one that is indicative of the kind of work you can do.

Describe a situation in which you had a difficult problem and how you solved it.

Relate one of your accomplishments, which had to do with this kind of situation. Depending on the organization's culture and needs, highlight conflict management, team building, or staffing.

As a manager, what do you look for when you hire people?

"Skills, initiative, accomplishments, creativity, adaptability - and whether their chemistry fits with that of the organization".

As a manager, have you ever had to fire anyone? If so, what were the circumstances and how did you handle it?

If you have, answer briefly that you have indeed had this experience and that it worked out to the benefit of both the individual and the organization. You followed the company's disciplinary procedures carefully before proceeding to termination. (The company may

Go to page 97 to get Liz Cassidy's personal help with your career

be concerned about discrimination and legal issues). Don't volunteer more information unless the interviewer asks for more details.

If you have never fired anyone, say so, but talk about how you would use performance management processes before resorting to termination, to protect the company's best interests.

What do you see as the most difficult task in being a (insert role title here)?

Your answer might address getting things done through others, getting things planned and completed on time within budget or maintaining high moral standards. Working with others is a valuable transferable skill – you might wish to work your abilities in this area into the discussion, if appropriate.

Describe some situations in which you have worked under pressure or met deadlines.

Refer to your accomplishments. Discuss one or two in which you were especially effective in meeting deadlines or dealing with high pressure situations.

Go to page 97 to get Liz Cassidy's personal help with your career

Tell me about an objective in your last job which you failed to meet and why.

> This question assumes that you failed to meet some of your objectives. If you can honestly state that you met all your established objectives, say so.

> If there was an objective that you were unable to meet for legitimate reasons, discuss it with an explanation of the obstacles over which you had no control. Even better, discuss an objective which you renegotiated when you realized it could not be met because of obstacles beyond your control.

What have you done that helped increase sales or profit? How did you go about it?

> This is your chance to describe in some detail a business accomplishment that is relevant to the proposed new position. Be specific about the numbers.

How much financial responsibility have you had in previous positions?

> You can answer this in terms of your budget, head count, or the size of the project or sales team that you directed. The more you can be specific, the more credible you are.

50

How many people have you managed in your recent positions?

Be specific - and feel free to refer to those over whom you had influence, such as a task force or a matrix organization.

Give examples of times when you were a leader.

Draw examples from accomplishments which demonstrate your leadership skills. Remember to keep all descriptions brief.

In your most recent position, what were some of your most significant accomplishments?

Since you have already selected the specific accomplishments you want to talk about, this question will be simple to answer. Be ready to describe three or four of them. When possible, try to relate your answer to the nature of the new challenges you might be facing.

If I spoke with your previous manager, what would he say are your greatest strengths (and/or weaknesses)?

Be consistent with what you think he would say. Position a weakness in a way which shows that you have worked on it. Use examples, not just words. Your former manager will probably want to give you a good reference, so recount

Go to page 97 to get Liz Cassidy's personal help with your career

some of the positive things you did for him or her.

Give one or two examples of your creativity.

Refer to accomplishments that relate to this position if possible.

Tell me about a time you faced an ethical dilemma.

The interviewer is looking for evidence of your ethical standards and honesty. Everyone has their ethics tested at some point. How you handle this question will show how you approach issues at large, e.g. you may have discovered a wrongdoing by a colleague, or someone asked you to engage in cutting corners.

Without naming names, describe the context and how you dealt with it.

Your political acumen and diplomacy are being tested with this question. Remember that questions you are asked in an interview are usually indicative of situations you will face in the role. This question has warning bells attached at many levels. Tread lightly in your response and be very tactful in your due diligence about the situation you may find yourself facing if you are offered the role.

Go to page 97 to get Liz Cassidy's personal help with your career

Give me proof of your technical competence.

How long is a piece of string?

This is a vague question which could be asked by a very clever interviewer or a hopelessly inadequate one. Err on the side of caution. Be clear, concise and firm in your response. It is useful to clarify in which particular skill area he wants reassurance, and then give examples of what you have done including your approach and your results.

He may follow up with a question about an area where you are not strong. Acknowledge this and state what you are doing to develop your skills in this area.

Go to page 97 to get Liz Cassidy's personal help with your career

"Will Do" Questions

What are your ambitions for the future?

Indicate your desire to concentrate on doing the immediate work well - and your confidence that the future will be promising. You do not want to convey that you have no desire to progress, but you need to avoid statements that are unrealistic, or that might threaten the present incumbent or that indicate you plan to leave after 2 years.

What do you know about our company?

If you have done your homework, you can honestly say that you have studied information that is publicly available about "ABC Limited" and are thus aware of many published facts. However, you might also state that you would like to know more; then be prepared to ask intelligent questions from your notes.

What things are most important to you in a work situation?

Use information developed from your Ideal Job reflections, and relate this to what you know about the position.

Go to page 97 to get Liz Cassidy's personal help with your career

Don't you feel you might be over qualified or too experienced for the position we have in mind?

Sometimes this questions means: "I am concerned that you are willing to take this position because you need to work and you will leave as soon as you get a better offer". Your answer must address this concern:

"You could be right, but having taken a voluntary early retirement from "DEF Company", I am in the fortunate position of being able to do what gives me the greatest satisfaction. And what I enjoy doing the most is" - (describe the contents of job).

It is also possible that you are getting the message, "Your salary expectation may be too high for the salary range of this position." Respond by mentioning your ability to "hit the ground running" and be "up to speed" quickly.

Tell me about a work situation that irritated you.

Talk about this type of situation in terms of the skills you used to manage and improve it. Avoid describing a work situation you know exists in your target company unless you want to emphasize that you can improve or eliminate

Go to page 97 to get Liz Cassidy's personal help with your career

it. Stress your ability to stay cool under pressure.

What important trends do you see coming in our industry?

Be prepared for this, do your homework.

Choose two or three important developments to discuss. This is an opportunity to show that you have thought about the future, the economics, the markets, the technology of the industry, and that you have done your research.

In your last position, what were the things that you liked the most? Liked least?

Respond with care to this question. You will want to emphasize the positives and place less emphasis on the negative elements.

What do you feel you should earn in this position?

You may want to answer this with a question such as "What is the typical compensation for similar positions in your company?" or "I consider my experience to be better than average, so I would expect to receive an offer that would be greater than the midpoint of the salary range for the position." If there is no range in the company, give the range that you

Go to page 97 to get Liz Cassidy's personal help with your career

had in mind. Qualify by saying you hope to learn more about the job scope and responsibilities.

What motivates you?

Keep your answer fairly general and as honest as you can, e.g. "The satisfaction of meeting the challenges of the position, developing teams and individuals, meeting organization goals." It is rarely appropriate to mention money as a motivator – unless in commission based sales.

What are your long range goals?

Relate your answers to their company rather than giving a very broad, general answer. Keep your ambitions realistic. Talk first about doing the work for which you are applying, and then talk about longer-range goals.

Tell me about a time when you failed.

No one is perfect and no one gets it right all the time. Talk about what you learned from a situation that went wrong. The interviewer will want to hear how you handled the fallout from any failures.

Tell a story that is not career limiting and also shows that you learned from the event.

Go to page 97 to get Liz Cassidy's personal help with your career

How will you tackle the first 90 days?

The interviewer may be testing how much you have thought about the job, but he is also looking for your thoroughness, your approach to process and your appreciation for the complexity of his business.

Maybe he will want more than the fact that you studied the company's business – this is expected of all candidates. Reassure him that you will work with the existing team and all key stakeholders to make sure that you are fully aware of all nuances of the role.

Be careful that you do not get specific on initiatives you want to take. Rather, let your responses show that you have a grasp of the size, scope and complexity of the role.

Go to page 97 to get Liz Cassidy's personal help with your career

"Best Fit" Questions

Tell me about yourself.

> This is your 2 Minute Introduction, and here
> you are building rapport and giving the
> interviewer a frame of reference.

What was your salary at "DEF Company"? What
kind of compensation are you looking for? How much
are you worth?

> This is very similar to the question in the last
> section.
>
> It is important to understand that organizations
> usually try to uncover your former salary to
> determine if the person is the right fit and to
> save them some money along the way. Instead,
> ask to defer this question until you have both
> assessed your fit for the role. This will position
> you as serious and considered. Deflecting your
> answer by saying that the "money is not as
> important as the responsibilities" and answers
> of that kind are regarded as stalling techniques
> and are not likely to be believed.
>
> If pressed then your best response is to answer
> with a question: "What is the range of this
> position?" or "What kind of salary does a

Go to page 97 to get Liz Cassidy's personal help with your career

person doing this work typically command in this organization?" If asked to elaborate further, you can say "During the last three years, my salary ranged from $_____ to $_____."

Why are you seeking a position with our company?

Indicate that from your study of the company, the business issues they face are the kind that excite you and match up well with your skills, abilities and past experiences. If you can do so honestly, express your admiration for the company and what it is that appeals to you.

How would you describe your personality?

Mention two or three of your most beneficial traits. To the extent that you can, highlight traits that would be a valuable asset to the work challenge under discussion. Remember that the interviewer is trying to determine your "fit" in the company, so your ability to accurately identify its corporate values will enable you to frame your response appropriately.

What is your sales/negotiation/conflict/management style?

No doubt you have an idea of your style already. Be prepared to describe yourself

Go to page 97 to get Liz Cassidy's personal help with your career

honestly in a way that shows you can work with others easily. You might want to talk about how you set goals and then get your people involved in them. Also, describe the techniques that you like to use to bring out the best in people, using the most appropriate style to fit the situation.

Your research may have given you a sense of whether the company believes in a highly participative style or is more authoritarian in its approach. If you do not know the company's style, keep your answer situational and refer to examples from your accomplishments.

Why are you leaving your present job?

This question must be answered briefly and without malice. If you get defensive or explain and rationalize to excess, you will only stir up questions and concerns in the interviewer's mind. If you are leaving due to a forced reduction due to economic circumstances, make that clear.

The interviewer wants to make sure you won't walk out after six months and that you'll be satisfied in your new position.

Go to page 97 to get Liz Cassidy's personal help with your career

Prepare a response you are comfortable with which shows you and your current employers in a positive light. Leaving to pursue your career goals and openness to new opportunities are generally safe.

Go to page 97 to get Liz Cassidy's personal help with your career

Describe what you feel would be an ideal work environment.

This is an opportunity to mention insights from your personal reflection - but don't make it sound too lofty or impractical. Refrain from mentioning any dis-satisfiers.

Looking back, how do you perceive your past employer?

Be positive. Refer to the valuable experience you have gained.

Never malign a former employer, no matter how justified.

Say something like, "It's an excellent company which has given me many valuable experiences and opportunities to perform successfully".

How do you think your subordinates/colleagues perceive you?

Be as positive as you can, referring to your strengths, skills and traits, but remember to be honest, too. References are easily checked.

Go to page 97 to get Liz Cassidy's personal help with your career

Why haven't you found a new position ... after so many months?

You may find this question offensive, but try not to take it personally.

Simply give a brief answer, "Finding any position in this marketplace is challenging, but finding the right position takes care and time," and move on.

What do you think of your previous manager?

This could be a loaded question. Be as positive as you can, and avoid becoming embroiled in the issue. If you like the individual, say so and why.

If you don't, think of something positive to say.

If we were to offer you this position, what changes would you make in our organization?

The timing of this question is important, since you can't give any specific answer without knowing some details about the position, organization and culture. Even if you do know, be careful about describing sweeping changes you might want to make.

Go to page 97 to get Liz Cassidy's personal help with your career

Do you have any objections to taking our battery of psychological tests?

They will only ask this question if they are serious about progressing with your application. Psychological tests are expensive. They are asking if it's okay to invest in you.

This is an indication that you are a serious candidate. There is only one sensible answer. "No, none at all."

What other types of work or companies are you considering at this time?

Don't feel obligated to reveal details of your other negotiations. If you are interviewing elsewhere refer to your campaign in a general way, but concentrate mainly on the specific position for which you are interviewing.

What are the recent movies you have seen?

Be honest. It's all right to show balanced interests by mentioning your viewing as well, so long as there is nothing too salacious or objectionable.

Go to page 97 to get Liz Cassidy's personal help with your career

What sort of relationships do you have with your associates, at the same level and above and below you?

This is an important question, so you will want to take the time to answer it in logical steps. When talking about your relationships with subordinates, be prepared to state your management philosophy, particularly with regard to performance issues.

When speaking of managers, indicate your keen interest in understanding your manager's expectations, so that you and your organization can build your goals in a way that will support his or her goals. You may also want to talk about how you will keep your manager informed. Stress your team building, mutually cooperative approach with peers.

What are some of your outside recreational activities?

Hopefully, your answer can show that you lead a balanced life. Avoid mentioning so many activities that you create doubt on how much time you will have for the job. Remember that your hobbies and recreational activities can be quite revealing about your own personality and values.

Go to page 97 to get Liz Cassidy's personal help with your career

Also be aware that your potential future employer is investing a lot of money into your salary. If your outside interests are high risk they may lose you to accident or injury. Be considered in your answer.

Go to page 97 to get Liz Cassidy's personal help with your career

What book are you currently reading?

The interviewer wants to find out if you are continuing to develop yourself, and if you are keeping up to date with your industry or profession.

The direct implication here is that you are actually reading. Be prepared to talk about a book, its concepts and your response or adoption of key ideas.

How do you describe your work style?

The interviewer is interested in finding out how you understand and articulate how you work.

Do you like structure, or flexibility? Do you like peace and quiet or do you thrive in chaos? The interviewer wants to see if you fit in the workplace.

Be prepared for this question by thinking about how you best operate. What is the best work environment to support how you prefer to work? Be specific and provide an example to support your description. It is entirely appropriate for you to ask the interviewer to describe what the workplace environment is like so that you can make an assessment of whether this is the best fit for you.

Go to page 97 to get Liz Cassidy's personal help with your career

Curve Ball Questions

If you were a superhero which one would you be?

Acknowledge the question as being ingenious...then think of your own skills and attributes to choose a superhero.

E.g. Iron man or batman use creativity and intelligence.
Thor uses blunt force.
Superman has an innate sense of justice.
Mr Incredible has a love of his family...
and so on.

Equally, you could be asked which animal or fairy tale character you are most like. The same approach applies.

"What is the meaning of life?"

Again the beauty and ugliness of this question is that the content of the answer is not relevant. What they are testing is how you can think on your feet, your graciousness and your mental agility.

Acknowledging the question to buy yourself time is useful. Once again, disarming honesty is the best bet, e.g. "I wish I knew that - it could save a lot of angst for a lot of people". If

Go to page 97 to get Liz Cassidy's personal help with your career

possible avoid nervous humour, as it may backfire.

"Tell me something that is not on your resume"

Ok this is not a question, but it certainly is a curve ball. Again you are being tested for mental agility. How you handle this with good humour and without making the interviewer look silly will test your tact and diplomacy.

Honest and innocuous would be suitable as a response here, e.g. I love my pet Labrador, or I like to walk on the beach, I went to an Adele concert before she had her operation, I read crime thrillers.

Some larger corporations are asking stretch questions to test your mental agility. If presented with one of these, take your time and consider the most simple response.

e.g. How do you weigh an elephant?

Put it on a barge and measure the change in water level on the outside of the boat. After you take the elephant off then add known weight to the boat to make the same depth change. Simple and obvious.

Go to page 97 to get Liz Cassidy's personal help with your career

Does this have anything to do with the role? Absolutely not, unless you are being interviewed for a Zoo or safari role.

The relevance of the curve-ball question is marginal – and you can consider this after the interview is complete when you are at home with friends.

What your interviewer may be trying to find out is how you think on your feet.

Go to page 97 to get Liz Cassidy's personal help with your career

Inappropriate Questions

When I was a young naïve engineer learning interview skills for a student recruitment campaign, our HR Manager grilled into us...

"Never ask an interview question of anyone that you would not ask of a white Anglo-Saxon, protestant, male."

That advice has stood me in good stead and to that list I would now add heterosexual, able bodied and in his prime.

When you put any candidate in this context there are a number of questions that don't need to be asked.

Unfortunately very few Managers got that same advice or exposure to the early training which I received.

As a result there are some well meaning but unaware interviewers who ask the silliest questions, often without realizing that the question itself may be "illegal".

Before we go any further, it's useful to acknowledge the difference between a question which is illegal and a question which could give rise to criminal liability.

Go to page 97 to get Liz Cassidy's personal help with your career

Most questions which taken at face value as "illegal" do not create a crime.

There is a vast difference between criminal liability and civil liability. For criminal liability to exist, there would be a motive or intent to commit a crime.

Most of the "illegal" questions I have heard and been asked are as a result of either ignorance or good intentions, they are not asked from malice. That is: ignorance of what is legal; ignorance of what questions are valid, and ignorance of how the answers might be misused in a discriminatory way.

There may still be civil liability even when there was no criminal intent.

So how do you respond when you have been asked an inappropriate question?

Given that most inappropriate questions are asked in innocence and ignorance, if you try to be politically correct then you will probably put the interviewer on guard and create an early end to the interview.

Examples of inappropriate question include:

> Are you planning a family?

> Are you planning to retire in the next few years?

Go to page 97 to get Liz Cassidy's personal help with your career

Do you need time off during the day to pray?

Are you pregnant?

Do you think you could cope as the only male in an all female workforce (or vice versa)?

How will you handle getting up and down the stairs with one leg? !!!!!

Does your religion prevent you from working weekends or holidays?

Do you have any use of your right arm at all?

Do you have any pre-existing health conditions?

So how can you be diplomatic and rescue the interview from falling off the cliff?

The choice is yours.

You may choose to be politically correct and assertive, correcting an obvious error and ending the interview (and this career opportunity), or

You can be brief and succinct in your answer and then change the subject, or

You can ignore the question and change the subject, or

Go to page 97 to get Liz Cassidy's personal help with your career

You can ask if there has been a previous issue in the organization which has caused the question to be asked, i.e. find out the real and underlying concern. Then you can alleviate it and show yourself to be caring, flexible and tactful.

E.g. Saying honestly, "There is nothing about my personal health or status that would get in the way of my performing well and doing a great job for you", will show you to be courteous and professional in the face of unprofessionalism.

Caveat

If you feel that you cannot perform the role for some reason, thank the interviewer for his/her time and move on to a role which you can do and which is a better fit for you.

Go to page 97 to get Liz Cassidy's personal help with your career

Beware of your need to be a hero

I have a very dear client who is a delightful person, a high achiever and outstanding employee.

Six years ago he accepted a role in an organization which had a totally different values set from him. He didn't fit, and the end of the employment was "messy". My client knew he was "in the right" and in his heightened emotional state sued the organization for unfair dismissal.

He won and it was a legal test case.

When you put his name into a search engine, the first 3 items are about his dismissal and the court case.

Now he is job hunting again and lives in stress that potential employers and recruiters will put his name into a search engine and find out his history. Note: he has done nothing wrong at all. But he is worried how his need to "win" legally six years ago could reflect on him today.

The reason for telling you this story is to give you pause to reflect if you are unfortunate enough to be asked inappropriate questions in an interview.

Do you want to be "RIGHT"? Or do you want have a stress free and successful career? If you choose to take a legal remedy to a real, or perceived, slight in an

Go to page 97 to get Liz Cassidy's personal help with your career

interview then as a minimum you will be buying into months of stress. Your name will also go into court documents and will be available to anyone who searches the internet looking for your history.

Go to page 97 to get Liz Cassidy's personal help with your career

Go to page 97 to get Liz Cassidy's personal help with your career

Chapter 9

Traps and Pitfalls

No matter how prepared we are most of us find job interviews stressful.

Under stress we can sometimes behave in a way we may regret later.

Again the best way to avoid regrets is to plan and practice in advance.

I have listed the most common pitfalls and traps for you to be prepared for and to make sure that you step around.

Being Unprepared

It seems so obvious. Get prepared. Do your research.

I have lost track of the number of people I have either interviewed or have coached for interview who seemed to think that they did not need to do any research about the organization they were planning to work for. At the very least visit their website. Put the

Go to page 97 to get Liz Cassidy's personal help with your career

company name into the news section of a search engine, and see what come up.

Look at what they talk about on their website:

What do they espouse as their values.

What is important to them?

Are they privately owned?

Are they a family business?

How many staff do they have?

Are they publicly listed?

Have they been in the news recently for anything good (or bad)?

How many countries are they in?

What is their product/service range?

Is this the kind of company you want to work for?

When you don't prepare for the interview you are sending a very clear message that

a) you don't care, or

b) you are lazy.

Go to page 97 to get Liz Cassidy's personal help with your career

In either case you are not a desirable candidate to them.

Talking too much

Our natural inclination is to avoid silence. A clever interviewer can use silence to create slight stress and cause you to talk too much. Be aware that sentences end with a period (full stop).

When you have finished making your point use the period to your advantage.

Finish speaking and hand the silence back to the interviewer to fill.

Waffling

This is a close cousin to talking too much. Take time to think through your answer then only answer the question asked. No more.

Swearing

No matter how coarse the interviewer may be, do not succumb to the trap of swearing.

Go to page 97 to get Liz Cassidy's personal help with your career

Being negative about your current/past employers

When you speak badly of your current or past employer, your interviewer will assume that you are a negative person. He will not want to spend time with you.

Being Late

A job interview is a business meeting.

Show up on time.

Enough said.

Asking About Benefits

While your interview is a due diligence opportunity, the negotiation side of what you will receive in return for your efforts (should you be successful) comes later.

The interviewer may ask you about your expectations to make sure you are in the right salary band. But you don't ask about salary/ flexible working hours / working from home/ crèche etc until you know they are seriously interested in you. That comes after the

Go to page 97 to get Liz Cassidy's personal help with your career

second interview, when you know they are going to invest time in reference checks.

Instead, use your interview to sell yourself so that they want to invest their dollars in you - not the other guy.

Turning Your Weaknesses Into Positives

When the interviewer asks you about your weakness be honest. Even the least trained interviewer knows bull dust when she hears it.

E.g. If you are interviewing for a sales role, tell them what your weaknesses are honestly, but be pragmatic about which weakness you choose. Time management as a weakness in this instance would be a deal breaker as it would impact on job performance.

However, being a beginner at using a spreadsheet (but you are taking night classes) would probably not hurt you with this role.

Lying

When you are keen to get a job there is an enormous temptation to mould your answers to fit what you believe the interviewer wants to hear. This is

Go to page 97 to get Liz Cassidy's personal help with your career

especially the case if you feel some rapport with the interviewer.

Avoid telling lies, even little white ones. If you get the job on the basis of a lie, there is a very real possibility that you are not a good fit and you will be unhappy. Equally there is a possibility that you will be found out at reference check and you will miss the opportunity.

Asking If There is Any Reason You Should Not Be Hired

When you ask this question the interviewer goes searching internally for an answer, and comes up with a reason why you should not be hired. This is simple psychology.

You are giving the interviewer an opportunity and an excuse not to hire you. It is a question which adds no value and does you great harm.

Looking too far in to the future

For your own peace of mind and to some control over your career it is important to know what your

Go to page 97 to get Liz Cassidy's personal help with your career

stepping stones are going to be. However your job interview is for this job, and this job only.

By all means show that you are interested in career advancement, but don't spend time focusing on it. More useful enquiries would be, "What are the criteria for success in this role?" and "Where has the person who had this role moved to?"

The answers to these questions will give you an insight into how the organization works.

Reacting to a Bad Interviewer

Many interviewers are just not trained. She may be busy, unfocussed, stressed, and unprepared.

She might do all the talking and forget to ask you questions. She may ask leading questions, e.g. "You're not very good at staying in jobs are you?" or might ask inappropriate questions.

She may not have read your resume and maybe does not have a copy available.

If you react to her lack of preparation or poor interview skills you will shorten the meeting and derail your opportunity (if you still want it).

Go to page 97 to get Liz Cassidy's personal help with your career

Instead, make her life easier. Have a copy of your resume available and offer to discuss some highlights which show that you are prepared and can address the needs of the role.

If the interviewer talks too much, don't cut her off. Simply take out your notepad and write keywords. Be attentive and listen carefully. When the opportunity presents itself use her keywords to present your experience to suit her needs.

Go to page 97 to get Liz Cassidy's personal help with your career

Chapter 10

Sample Questions to Ask at the Interview

Be prepared to ask your own questions – after all, this is a two way exploration. Select from the questions below those that are most appropriate for your situation, and add your own questions that are unique to your circumstances and to the position at hand.

Why is the position open?

How often has this role been filled in the past two/five years?

Why did the person most recently in this job leave?

What would you like done differently by the next person who does this work?

What are some of the objectives you would like accomplished - short term and long term?

What is the most pressing? What would you like to have accomplished within the next two or three months?

What freedom would I have to determine my work objectives, deadlines and methods of measurement?

Go to page 97 to get Liz Cassidy's personal help with your career

What kind of support does this position receive in terms of people and budget?

What are some of the more difficult problems facing someone in this position? How do you think these could be best handled?

Where could a person who is successful in this position go, and within what time frame?

What significant changes do you foresee in the near future?

How is one evaluated? What accounts for success?

What are the most critical factors for success in your business?

Where do you see the company (or function) going in the next few years?

How do you win support from top management?

How would you describe your own management style?

What are the most important traits you look for?

How do you prefer your staff to communicate with you? (Orally, in writing, informally, in meetings, only when necessary?). How often?

Go to page 97 to get Liz Cassidy's personal help with your career

Describe the team culture that this role fits into.

Who are the significant stakeholders who interact with this role? What are their primary concerns?

What are the idiosyncrasies of the role that have not been covered so far?

All these questions draw out more information about the company and the role. The answers will be insightful and help you in your discovery process.

The answers will help you to answer the question "Do I want this job?"

Go to page 97 to get Liz Cassidy's personal help with your career

Go to page 97 to get Liz Cassidy's personal help with your career

Chapter 11

Closing

For your own peace of mind, pay attention to closure at the end of the interview. Because there is usually a great feeling of relief many people do not ask the few simple questions that can remove some of the anxiety in the weeks following.

Take note of the following questions. Bring them with you and make sure you leave enough time at the end of the interview to collect this information. These questions can also be asked as you are walking out with the interviewer or are preparing to leave.

Required Questions

What arc the next steps?

What is the timing?

Where am I in the interview sequence?

Will there be additional rounds of interviews?

When will you notify the candidates?

Go to page 97 to get Liz Cassidy's personal help with your career

Go to page 97 to get Liz Cassidy's personal help with your career

Chapter 12

Follow Up

I suggest that you write a thank you note within 24 hours, expressing your pleasure and interest in the role.

Unless it is an unusual circumstance, thank you letters/cards should be no longer than one page, and they should contain something that causes the recipient to remember you, weaving in information that is work related.

Avoid emails. Make yourself stand out from the crowd: write a handwritten note on quality white paper or on a classy greeting card.

If you noticed that the interviewer had an issue with something you discussed, bring it up in the thank you letter with a possible solution or verification. You can start the paragraph with "Upon further reflection, I feel that…."

Send individualized thank you letters to everyone with whom you interviewed on a one to one basis - say something a little different to each person.

Go to page 97 to get Liz Cassidy's personal help with your career

It is not necessary to send individual letters to everyone in a panel interview. However, you will know through your closure questions which individuals you need to follow up with. Send a letter to that person and also to the decision maker if they are different people.

Ensure that your handwriting is legible.

Analysing Progress

As with any strategy implementation, careful recording of results allows you to monitor your progress to your target outcome.

Use a journal/diary to monitor and plan time spent on your recruitment project.

Record the outcomes from each contact and interview.

This analysis is important in assessing your need for further practice or training. Be honest with yourself. It is possible to invest months in interview preparation and sacrifice the job in the interview. Learn from each experience and use your cumulative learning to continuously improve your interviewing skills.

- The following post interview checklist will help you to analyse your performance:
- What went well? Why?
- What did not go well? Why?

Go to page 97 to get Liz Cassidy's personal help with your career

- What would I do differently if I were to repeat the interview?
- What are my key lessons?
- What interview skills must I develop further?

As a lifelong learner the more you can pin point and change what didn't work, while leveraging off what you did well, the faster you will get to your goal.

It is important to complete your post analysis as soon as possible after each interview with a view to learning and improvement, not with the goal of self-flagellation.

After each interview check your notes and check the answers provided to your discovery questions.

- How close is this role to your ideal?
- What will you have to compromise on if you accept this role?
- What will be the unintended consequences of accepting the role?
- Do I still want the role?

Go to page 97 to get Liz Cassidy's personal help with your career

If after reviewing all these questions and your follow up research you decide that this role in this organization suits you in your career plan, then I wish you …

Good luck

Go to page 97 to get Liz Cassidy's personal help with your career

Get Liz Cassidy's Personal Help

Could you be sabotaging yourself at work?

Sometimes we are doing things which hold our careers back which others can clearly see, but which we are blind to.

These wholly unconscious behaviours can derail your career.

When you take the Online Apollo Behavioral Profile then you get a clear report of what you are doing well, what you need to be aware of and clear Red traffic lights on what areas you could be sabotaging yourself.

Go to *http://tinyurl.com/ApolloProfile* to order your Behavioral Profile.

Liz Cassidy will organise an exclusive 1 hour private phone debrief of your profile to get you back on track to get the best from your next career move.

Go to page 97 to get Liz Cassidy's personal help with your career

Other Resources From Liz Cassidy

Are you using your own professional network to help you find a new job?

If not, you could be missing out on hundreds of unadvertised roles.

Learn how to build your career through building and using your network with **"Business Networking Success"** by Liz Cassidy via Amazon

Avoid Career Stress And Mistakes:

Become very clear about what you stand for , know your "true north".

Check if the organizations values align with yours. Download **"Living Your Values Centred Life"** by Liz Cassidy

Go to http://tinyurl.com/ValuesEbook

Go to page 97 to get Liz Cassidy's personal help with your career

www.ingramcontent.com/pod-product-compliance
Lightning Source LLC
Chambersburg PA
CBHW071238170526
45165CB00003B/1156